Moving Beyond Grief

HOW TO SHIFT FROM GRIEF AND LOSS TO JOY AND PEACE

Lucy Appadoo

"As a counsellor specialising in grief, bereavement and trauma I work with many women who struggle to understand the impact of their grief, and find meaning in their life beyond loss.

Lucy Appadoo's "How to Shift from Grief and Loss to Joy and Peace" offers both a courageous personal story of transformation through a parent's worst nightmare in the death of a child, and accessible psycho-education and strategies to assist anyone attempting to make sense of their grief experience. This humble and informative book would be a positive companion to professional women both personally and professionally. This amazing resource is accessible to both professional and personal audiences, and captures the heart of self compassion that is central to healing, transformation and a joyous life. In reading this book you will be both touched deeply, resourced with tools to work through grief and loss, and left with hope on your ongoing life.

Thank you for your courage and insight Lucy."

Jenny Field
Counsellor and Clinical Supervisor JField Counselling

"Lucy's ability to interpret the key steps of grief is profoundly moving and uplifting. She allows the reader to experience her trauma first-hand and shows us the human side of what it feels like to let go of a loved one regardless of how long we have known them. The grief and loss book is a book that I highly recommend for all of us to read because it is part of our life journey. We will all experience this in our life, and having this knowledge of what to expect makes the experience less daunting. I was moved by Lucy's personal story as it really resonated with me the stages of grief and how I felt when my mum passed six years ago. Lucy's story is cathartic and life-changing. This book is a must-have on your bookshelf or digital book catalogue."

Suzanne (Musster) Marambio
Mindfulness Facilitator and Co-Founder

"This is a very readable, practical guide to processing grief and loss. Broken down into three succinct sections, it invites the reader to expand their knowledge around grief, to bear witness to the authors own very personal story of grief and loss and concludes with lots of useful tools, strategies and resources to assist them to work through these very difficult emotions. As a Counsellor working with many professional women, as well as those bereaved by suicide, I'd confidently recommend this book as a wonderful way to gain more understanding around grief and it's processes."

Janene Warren
Women's Counsellor and Suicide Response Team Member.

"As a physiotherapist who just lost my father one year ago, this book helped me to understand that grief is normal and something we work through, not suppress. As healthcare providers, we are always taking care of others, but this book encourages you to closely examine and be gentle on yourself. Lucy's knowledge, case studies, and personal stories make this book so relatable. It made me realize that the way through grief is to embrace it and find courage through others' vulnerable stories. Her solution-focused approach to moving through grief also gave me the tools to use in my own life and in coping with the loss of my father."

Jennifer George
Physiotherapist, Consultant to Health Professionals and Mentor to students on Influential Communication in Healthcare.

Copyright © 2019 by Lucy Appadoo. All Rights Reserved.

No part of this publication may be reproduced, distributed, or transmitted in any form or by any means, including photocopying, recording, or other electronic or mechanical methods, or by any information storage and retrieval system without the prior written permission of the publisher, except in the case of very brief quotations embodied in critical reviews and certain other non-commercial uses permitted by copyright law.

This book is for informational purposes only and is not intended as a substitute for the advice and care of your health provider. As with all health advice, please consult with a doctor to make sure this resource is appropriate for your individual circumstances. The author and publisher expressly disclaim responsibility for any adverse effects that may result from the use or application of the information contained in this book.

This book is dedicated to our beautiful son, Jared, who never got the chance to grow up. We will always love you, our beautiful boy.

TABLE OF CONTENTS

Introduction 1
How To Use This Book 3
Part One: Educational Components Of Grief And Loss 4
Part Two: Personal Touch.. 20
Part Three: Solutions For Moving Beyond Grief.......................... 35
Conclusion 42
Books/Resources... 43
Resources For The Community 44
About The Author... 45
Also By Lucy Appadoo 46

Introduction

Moving Beyond Grief - How to Shift from Grief and Loss to Joy and Peace helps professional women who are struggling with grief to move forward to joy and peace and aspire to greater things after the loss of a loved one or something important. This book focuses on the educational aspects of grief and loss, case studies, and solutions for moving beyond grief. I would like to inspire others to understand grief and move beyond loss.

Grief is a normal reaction to loss. It varies from person to person and affects your emotions, behaviours, thoughts, physical body, spiritual perspective, and social or work environment. Grief can shatter your previously-held view of the world and especially impacts the frontal cortex part of the brain that helps you to plan, focus, and make decisions. It is therefore wise not to make huge decisions while your grief is raw and acute.

You can get stuck in the grief process when you don't accept the reality of the loss. You continue to yearn for what you lost. If you are grieving the loss of a loved one, you cannot think of your loved one without deep sorrow and pain. You have lost your sense of self, and your connection to others and life has ceased to exist. If you don't work through these issues, you can develop complicated grief. Complicated grief is unresolved grief due to complications that hinder the mourning process. This happens when you cannot acknowledge the finality of the death and have lost any ability to gain meaning or purpose from the loss.

Alternatively, acute grief is a normal human process and impacts you if you had a deep attachment to the person or thing of importance. The mourning process is crucial to moving forward from the loss.

Grief is a response to many losses, including the loss of a spouse, child, friend, sibling, other family member, or a pet. You can also grieve the loss of something important in your life such as a job, relationship, home, and so forth. The grief can become even more complicated if the loss of a loved one was due to suicide or homicide.

Self-compassion is caring for yourself despite your faults or weaknesses or especially during times of emotional distress. It is identifying with your own humanity, imperfections and all. Self-compassion is central to healing when you are grieving and allows you to become more present to yourself. You need to identify your pain and suffering and be open to it, rather than fight the sadness and loss. Only with self-compassion can you show yourself kindness without self-judgement, without feeling isolated, and without over-identifying with your pain. Self-compassion allows you to notice that loss is a shared human experience. You can take a break from negative ruminations and find more balance between allowing pain and getting on with your day-to-day tasks so you can live a lot more in the moment.

The approaches I use in this book are current and valid, and I have used these strategies with former clients experiencing grief and loss. The strategies that will work for you will depend on your grieving style, that is, whether you prefer to grieve alone (instrumental griever) or whether you prefer to grieve with others (intuitive griever). Both grieving styles will be discussed later in the book.

This is a book to help you move towards joy and peace after loss. It will help you manage time, find your passion, overcome anxiety, and take greater care of yourself.

Part One of the book covers the educational aspects of grief and loss, including the impacts of grief, the different styles of grieving, and strategies to help you move forward after grief and loss.

Part Two focuses on my personal struggle with grief and loss. I also present two case studies of grief and loss related to two clients I previously counselled.

Part Three focuses on the practical aspects of grief and loss, including how to use your inner strengths and external resources to move beyond grief, how to create a future vision of wellness or area of change, and how to create a life that is meaningful and brings you joy and peace.

The final section outlines tools and resources you can use, including my own products or books.

How to Use This Book

The best way to use this book is by reading the section on the educational aspects of grief first so the solutions and practicalities will make more sense. However, if you have some understanding of grief and loss, you might wish to skip some parts and read what is most relevant and interesting for you. I hope you enjoy the book journey from start to finish.

PART ONE:

Educational Components of Grief and Loss

What is Grief?

I can recall a year of what I perceived as insurmountable odds when I received one lot of bad news after another. I had my both of my siblings fall ill, followed by my father, and then my mother. I struggled to cope with their sickness and wondered why all my family members were getting sick. I wondered if I would be next. My body went into shock, and I got this sense of unreality and surrealness as if I wasn't even inside my body. I didn't want to be inside my body because of the pain and loss I had experienced knowing my family members would not be functioning as they once had. I hadn't experienced death, but the loss had great meaning. I responded by grieving for who my family members once were. My stable world was shattered, because I did not know whether they would get sicker or recover. Luckily they recovered.

The Collins Australian Dictionary defines grief as *deep or intense sorrow* or *something that causes keen distress*. Grief is a reaction to a range of losses, and the response to loss can vary for each person. The loss might be related to the death of a loved one, including a family member or friend, or it might be related to the loss of something, including health, a job, a relationship, or identity. Grief consists of a range of emotions and behaviours that are common after a loss of someone or something.

Mourning refers to the process of grieving the death of a loved one. According to J.W. Worden (Grief Counselling and Grief Therapy, 2009), the mourning process goes through four tasks:

Task 1: To Accept the Reality of the Loss

During this stage, you feel as if the death hasn't occurred even if it was expected. For this task, you need to come to terms with and accept the death. A sense of yearning occurs during this stage. You may believe the deceased is walking down the street or is somewhere else. You later realise your loved one is actually dead and will never return.

When my son Jared died, I was numb and in shock. I couldn't believe my son had died when I had all these expectations and dreams and had prepared the nursery for him at home. I never expected he would stop breathing, and I wondered if I could have done anything different. It was a difficult stage to get through, but I got through it with the help of family and friends.

Task 2: To Process the Pain of Grief

Grief involves emotional and physical pain, so it is essential that you validate and work through this pain. Avoiding the emotion of pain can manifest in physical symptoms or behaviour that is abnormal in that it goes against the socialised way of behaving or prevents you from functioning day to day. If you don't work through the pain by validating, accepting, and being true to your emotions, you delay the mourning process. However, everyone's level of pain is different after loss and is dependent on the kind of attachment you had to the deceased.

I struggled with my emotions and yearned for my son after his death. I was able to work through my emotional pain (sadness, yearning, emptiness) and physical pain (aches and pain in my body and an inability to sleep) by processing my emotions when writing his biography, creating a memory box, arranging his photos, reading about death, and talking to friends and family. These rituals allowed me to work through the grief period.

Task 3: To Adjust to a World Without the Deceased

Worden outlines three areas of adjustment you need to work through after the death of a loved one. These include external adjustment, internal adjustments, and spiritual adjustment.

External adjustment refers to adapting to a new environment without your loved one, which depends on your level of attachment to the deceased. Deaths of those we're close to lead to secondary losses. For instance, a woman who has lost her husband needs to adapt to a world of raising her children alone, living alone, managing money alone, or coming to terms with an empty house. If the husband managed the finances, the woman may need to learn to do this herself. She may also lose financial stability due to loss of her husband's wage. She may experience loss of security and the loss of her identity as a wife as well. It usually takes three to four months to adjust to secondary losses.

The death of my son meant I had to adjust to lack of motherhood and the lack of a nurturing role. I had to adapt to a life without a child and needed to consider what to do about the nursery. It was the worst time of my life, but I had to eventually live my life and move on or I'd be forever stuck in the past.

Internal adjustment refers to adapting to your own sense of self. In other words, how the death influences your self-esteem and capabilities. For instance, if as a woman you see your identity or role through relationships and caring for others, you would experience not only the loss of your loved one but also the loss of self or identity. You might wonder who you are now that you are not a carer or a wife. Also, you may wonder about your abilities or self-efficacy when you struggle to take over your loved one's role, such as financial tasks.

I personally questioned whether I did something wrong while I was pregnant and wondered why Jared stopped breathing. Did I exert myself too much while I was pregnant? I blamed myself for his death until I was able to see sense. I questioned who I was when I was no longer a mother.

Spiritual adjustment refers to the loss of your values and philosophical beliefs, which are beliefs influenced by family, friends, education, religion, and life experiences. You might lose your direction in life and seek to find meaning in the loss as you've now lost control. For example, when a mother has lost her child, she will question why God let this happen as her belief might be that children shouldn't die before their parents. The adjustment is worse when a loved one is missing as you don't know whether the person is alive or dead somewhere.

Task Three is about establishing new skills to cope, facing the world anew, and becoming more independent and confident to gain a new sense of yourself and the world.

I wondered why God would let my son die before me. That wasn't the rule of life. I was angry with the world and lost my joy for life. It was cold, dark, and empty, and I wondered why life could be so cruel that an innocent child would die before his parents.

Task Four: To Find an Enduring Connection With the Deceased Amidst Embarking On A New Life

This is the stage when you develop a continuing bond with your loved one. In other words, you can remain connected to the deceased through rituals, memories, or anniversaries and still move forward with your life.

I visit Jared's cemetery, light a candle on his birthday, look at his photos, conjure my memories of him from time to time, and talk to my children and family on the anniversary of his death and Christmas. He'll always be a part of my life as he was my very first child who remains forever in my heart.

Bereavement is the actual experience of the loss of a close loved one and does not refer to other losses. The timing of bereavement is different for everyone.

In terms of the bereavement experience, things can get worse after some time has passed and your family and friends have stopped visiting. You suddenly feel worse as you need to adjust to the changes. There are no longer distractions, but over time you can learn to adjust. Particular experiences will trigger your feelings of loss, so you will experience the pain in cycles over the course of your life.

The Impacts of Grief

Processing Grief is like treasure hunting in the dump. In order to find the good stuff, you can't tiptoe through. You must dig in and prepare to get messy, knowing the riches of joy and peace lie underneath the unpleasant stuff (www.lorilara.com)

Grief impacts all areas of your life, and includes the following:

Emotions

Emotions after the death of a loved one may include sadness, anger that the deceased had to die and leave you, yearning, guilt, anxiety, a sense of helplessness, shock, relief (if your loved one was suffering), loneliness, flat affect, and tiredness. Some people might express anger towards God if they have religious or spiritual beliefs and cannot make sense of the death.

Thoughts

Grief impacts the frontal cortex of the brain or executive skills, including the ability to plan, focus, or make decisions. That's why it's advisable never to make big decisions while grieving. You will also tend to ruminate, engage in obsessive thoughts about the deceased, and question why this happened. You might engage in absolute thinking, saying 'it's all my fault,' as the brain works overtime during the grief process.

You may also tell yourself this death has not happened, especially after a sudden death. In other words, you have a sense of disbelief and a freeze response. You might sense the presence of the deceased, particularly after the death of a child. Your loved one might be offering you a level of comfort and peace. I know I had this sense of presence after my baby son died, and I felt comforted by it.

Research has shown that 50 percent of those with spiritual beliefs cope better with grief than those without spiritual beliefs.

Physical

Grief can give rise to physical symptoms. During grief, your body creates chemicals designed to reduce your pain to a tolerable level. This is why your body is in shock after hearing that your loved has died, and you feel numb. These chemicals can be released through tears or for some, through exercise. Over time, the chemicals subside, but your emotional distress increases because you have a stronger awareness of the death (a reality check). During this reality check, your body will cope by creating more chemicals through tears to help with survival. You can feel better after a flood of tears.

Physical symptoms can include an emptiness in the stomach, tightness in the throat and chest, a lack of energy, a feeling that nothing in your environment is real, symptoms of anxiety such as dry mouth and shortness of breath, an inability to cope with noise or chaos, and muscle weakness.

During grief, you might also experience stomach problems, skin issues, indigestion, migraines, chest pain, or muscle spasms.

Behaviours

You may have a reduced appetite while grieving (which is more common than overeating), and you may struggle to sleep due to the stress chemical adrenalin you produce so that you can cope. Adrenalin is a hormone produced by the adrenal glands and can give you a surge of energy. However, too much of this hormone can impact your health (heart, brain, and other organs).

You may withdraw from friends and family at the acute grief stage as you might believe others don't understand your loss and emotionally you are not in that headspace to have fun, talk, and entertain others. You might also be sick and tired of others telling you 'I'm sorry' or 'You're so strong.'

It's common to have dreams or nightmares of your loved one, depending on where you are at the grief stage. For instance, if you're feeling guilty or remorseful, you might dream about symbols or an event representing these emotions to work through the issues. You might also dream of your loved one for comfort or due to lack of closure (unfinished business with the deceased).

Other behaviours during the grief process include crying, avoiding or seeking reminders of the loss, absentmindedness (for instance, you cannot remember doing a certain activity), accidents, increases in drinking alcohol, smoking or other substance use, difficulty attending work in the short-term, and constant searching for your loved one (if you're struggling to accept the loss or are in the acute stage)

Spiritual or Philosophical Perspectives of the World

Spirituality comes into play when you work to understand the meaning and purpose of life. You might question why God took away your young child or young family member when life doesn't take its natural course in terms of death at an old age. Your beliefs might be challenged, or they may not be if your loved one lived a long, quality life.

Loss generally leads to questioning your spiritual or religious beliefs due to an attempt to make sense of the loss. Your world is turned upside down as your identity is challenged. Your assumptions about the world tend to change too as the pain can lead to a sense of insecurity and a realistic perception of mortality.

Grieving Styles

The tide recedes but leaves behind bright seashells on the sand.
The sun goes down, but gentle warmth still lingers on the land.
The music stops, and yet it echoes on in sweet refrains...
For every joy that passes, something beautiful remains.
Remember her...
Speak of her...
Mention her...
(Author unknown - from The Australian Centre for Grief & Bereavement)

The different grieving styles are intuitive and instrumental. If you grieve with a mixture of both styles, you have a blended grief style.

Intuitive grievers prefer to grieve in the following ways:
- Social - Prefer sharing their grief with others.
- Affective - Prefer to express grief by crying.
- Passive - Prefer to be with the grief and not do anything about it.
- Focused on the past and present - Are not planning things in relation to the grief.

Instrumental grievers prefer to grieve in the following ways:
- Solitary - Prefer to grieve on their own.

- Thought-Oriented - Ruminate about the grief and question why it happened and what happened. They experience feelings less intensely than intuitive grievers.
- Action-Oriented - They prefer doing and like to fix things. They are very practical and may make things such as a plaque or plant a tree to honour the person lost. People with this style may also prefer to discuss problems rather than feelings.
- Focused on the future - Prefer to plan and may do things related to the loss, such as resolving financial issues or sorting out belongings.

Generally, intuitive grievers are comfortable in the acute stages of grief, but instrumental grievers appear not to be grieving as they don't express their emotions. These choices of how to grieve are the person's adaptive strategies, though most grievers use a blend of intuitive and instrumental grief. Despite a blended style, most grievers do prefer one style over the other. Instrumental grievers can find an outlet for their emotions, even if they're not as intense as intuitive grievers' emotions, by expressing them through planned activities such as creating a monument for the deceased, while intuitive grievers can struggle to simply think about their emotions without deeply feeling them.

Without an understanding of the different grieving styles, miscommunication and misunderstanding can occur among families or friends. It's important to realise that people do grieve in different ways, and that is okay.

What determines people's grieving styles?

Both cultural factors (based on upbringing and traditional beliefs of the family and social environment) and personality play a role in how people respond to grief, whether intuitive or instrumental. If the meaning of the loss is significant, you will grieve in your own way. The way you grieve also depends on how well you can control or regulate your emotions or your level of resilience.

A final factor is gender role socialisation. In other words, as children grow into men, they may have more of a preference for an instrumental grieving style, while women tend to be more intuitive due to the way they are socialised and gender roles. However, even though grieving styles are influenced by gender, they are not determined by gender, so it's best not to assume that a man will be an instrumental griever and a woman an intuitive griever.

Five Strategies to Help You with Grief

These grief strategies came from a workshop I attended with Robert. A. Neimeyer, a psychologist and grief expert from the United States. I have used these tasks with my own clients. The strategies involve a few methods of journal writing.

1. Directed Journalling

Directed Journalling for Emotional Exploration
- Find somewhere private.
- Focus on your deepest thoughts and feelings.
- Don't concern yourself with grammar or spelling and write only for yourself.
- Write for 20 minutes a day for at least four days.
- Organise an activity afterwards to return to your normal day.
- Have a support person or professional on hand if needed.
- When you start writing, respond to questions such as: How did you respond to the event at the time? Put yourself back in that moment of hearing the news of the death. How did your feelings about the loss change over time? What was the most emotionally significant aspect of the loss for you?

Directed Journalling for Sense-Making

Respond to the following questions in your journal:
- How did you make sense of the death at the time? How do you make sense of the death now?
- What philosophical or spiritual beliefs influenced the way you coped? How were your beliefs influenced by the death?
- How has the death impacted your direction in life? How have you dealt with this over time?
- How, in the long-term, do you imagine you will give this death meaning in your life?

Directed Journalling for Benefit-Finding

Respond to the following questions in your journal:
- In your opinion, have you found any gifts in your grief? If so, what?
- How has this death impacted your priorities?
- What qualities in yourself have you utilised to help you with your resilience?
- What qualities of a supportive style have you found in others?
- What lessons about loving did your loved one teach you?
- Has this huge adjustment increased your gratitude for anything you've been given? If so, to whom can you express this gratitude?

2. Use of Rituals to Honour the Loss

Grief rituals are regular or repeated tasks performed to honour your loved one. They are a powerful method used to help you cope with loss and are best performed after you've passed the acute grief stage when your emotions have somewhat settled.

Rituals are powerful as they help you deal with the loss by using your conscious and unconscious minds. In other words, they work on a deep level to help you move forward with life. They provide you with a safe space to confront the grief in a contained way. They help you symbolise your love and memory of the deceased and can provide closure during a dark time.

Rituals tend to vary and can provide a continuing bond or connection with the deceased. They signify a transition in your grief process, honour the deceased, and acknowledge your relationship with your loved one or create closure if you had an ambivalent relationship with the deceased. Rituals can also form a part of your religion, spiritual beliefs, or cultural beliefs. Furthermore, rituals can be performed on your own or as part of a group or community (for example, a funeral).

Rituals come in various forms, according to Kenneth Doka (Therapeutic Ritual, Ch 87 in *Techniques of Grief Therapy*, 2012). For example, Rituals of Continuity demonstrate that you still remember your loved one. An anniversary mass is one such example and may be a yearly occurrence.

Another type of ritual is a Ritual of Transition, which serves to demonstrate that you have journeyed to a new place in your grief. For example, you might give away your loved one's clothing, which shows you have moved forward from the loss.

A Ritual of Reconciliation is performed to show forgiveness towards your loved one if you had a conflicted relationship. For example, you might write a letter to your father to show forgiveness for his previous neglect.

The final ritual is a Ritual of Affirmation that you perform to show a way of giving thanks or acknowledging a legacy. For example, you might wish to say thank you to your mother for providing you with a godmother to help you through life.

Rituals can be performed during the anniversary of a death, a yearly celebration (Christmas or Easter), or your loved one's birthday. Here are examples of general rituals you can perform:

- an anniversary mass or memorial service to honour your loved one.
- writing a letter to your loved on to say thank you or develop closure.
- lighting a candle to honour the memory on an anniversary or birthday.
- listening to your loved one's favourite music.
- engaging in a comforting prayer.
- visiting the grave of your loved one and bringing flowers.
- creating a small shrine in the home and taking comfort in this place during special times.

In summary, rituals provide a way of coping with loss and can be repetitive in nature. They offer a symbolic act and can provide you with a measure of comfort and acknowledgement of the loss. Rituals can be ongoing, temporary, transitioning, forgiving, or affirming.

3. Self-Care and Relaxation Methods

You can easily forget basic self-care tasks when you are grieving. Especially, if you have a health condition, self-care is important. Basic self-care includes eating a healthy diet that contains all the essential nutrients, including protein, dairy, carbohydrates, fruits and vegetables, and regular fluid intake. Even if you're not hungry, you can graze on light snacks if your stomach cannot tolerate full meals.

Here are a range of ideas for self-care and relaxation during grief:
- Take a moment to soak in the sunlight.
- Go for a pleasant walk and explore your surroundings.
- Watch a funny movie or show, as laughter is therapeutic.
- Enjoy a massage.
- Listen to relaxing music and close your eyes, focusing on your breathing for at least ten minutes.
- Engage in moderate exercise to release any tension or stress in the body.
- Find ways you've previously relaxed and cared for yourself. Do whatever works for you. For example, some people might find going out relaxes them while others might find spending time in solitude will recharge their batteries. Find self-care and relaxation activities that work for your individual style and temperament.

Relaxation Exercise

This short relaxation exercise was taken from Leah Giarratano's book, *Managing Psychological Trauma* (2004):

1. Sit or lie down in a comfortable place and close your eyes.
2. Select the colour that is most relaxing and calming for you.
3. Notice your breathing and start to breathe slowly in and out.
4. Imagine a light over your head. This light is your soothing and relaxing colour. Each time you inhale, imagine some of this light washing over your body.
5. Imagine that as each part the light touches you, it calms and relaxes you. Each time you breathe in, more and more light washes over your body. See it washing over your forehead and eyes, feeling it calm and relax you, over your jaw and neck, soothing and calming wherever the colour touches you. Continue seeing the light move throughout your body.

6. This light comes from an endless source, and the more light you breathe in, the more light is available. Breathe in more and more light, more and more, more and more.

4. Relationships and Communication

A useful tool you can use when grieving is a tool grief therapists Kenneth Doka and Robert A.Neimeyer describe in chapter 80 of *Techniques of Grief Therapy - Creative Practices for Counselling the Bereaved* (2012). The chapter, titled 'Orchestrating Social Support', focuses on relationships and communication with others during the grieving process. The tool is known as the DLR Tool, which stands for the Doer, the Listener or the Respite figure. In the exercise, you identify people who play each of those roles in your life. When you complete the exercise, you can also use an X to indicate a negative or destructive relationship with one of the people you have identified. You can also journal this information for yourself. To do this, determine who in your life falls into the following groups:

- Doers (D): People you can rely on to get tasks done, such as housework or other practical tasks.
- Listeners (L): Friends who listen and provide support and don't necessarily give you advice or criticise you, but simply listen to how you feel and think.
- Respite Figures (R): Supportive friends or family members with whom you can do specific activities for sheer enjoyment, like exercising or going to a museum.
- Negative or Destructive Figures (X): People who are best to avoid. If you need to interact with them (for example, if they're a critical parent or relative), then have minimal interaction with these people.

1. You can start off by writing a list of your support system, including friends, family, colleagues, school, religious environment, and other interest groups.
2. Identify people under each category of D, L, R, X, realising that some people may slot into a range of categories. You can acknowledge your top five or six people in each category.

3. Arrange an interaction with at least one, D, L, and R person weekly.
4. Recognise the strengths of each person. For instance, those with great handyman skills (a doer) might not be great company for a performance (a respite figure). Furthermore, a respite person might not be comfortable with strong emotions, hence you also need a listener figure.
5. Acknowledge what type of person you need during grief and be assertive.
6. Be assertive with those people who are critical or clingy. Minimise your time with negative or destructive figures.
7. Take time out talking about the loss to have a balance between sadness and respite.

It's a good idea to interact with a range of people from the groups above so that one person doesn't bear too much responsibility and burn out. Seeking out a range of activities with those who fulfil a specific need can help you move forward. You will always need help with practical matters. You might need someone to simply listen to your feelings and thoughts, or you might need someone to enjoy a pleasant outing with.

While you are grieving, it is important to explain to family and friends exactly what you need. At times, you might not wish to offend a person, but you are the one grieving and you are the one who has needs at this sensitive time. Communicate exactly what you need and be assertive. If you struggle to communicate your needs clearly and find that you're sacrificing your own needs, you may wish to seek the help of a grief counsellor or trusted friend.

Relationships change. Family dynamics change during this grief journey. Your role within your family will change and your energy will deplete, so give yourself the time and space you need. Instrumental grievers may not wish to share their feelings with others but may like help with an activity like planting a tree in honour of the deceased. Intuitive grievers, however, need to share exactly what they're feeling during the grieving process.

5. Coping with holidays and special celebrations

Holidays and celebrations can be met with a lot of nervous anticipation and dread as your loved one is not there to share this time with you. Memories come flooding back, and you feel the absence of your loved one.

Christmas, Easter, anniversaries of the death of your loved one, holidays, and other special events are trying times. These times increase the reality of your loss, and you might struggle to laugh and enjoy yourself during these events.

Here are a range of tips to better manage special occasions and holidays:
- Make plans. By getting organised in advance, you can avoid anxiety. Do what feels right for you.
- Give yourself permission to grieve and have a cry. Let others know how you're feeling and gain a supportive ear.
- Share your plans with friends and family. Follow what's right for your immediate family rather than feel pressure from others. Let others know how you feel and what you need during the occasion.
- Honour your loved one in a particular way, such as lighting a candle for them on Christmas Day or hanging a special ornament with their name on it on your Christmas tree. You might visit a church and spend time reminiscing with fond memories, or you might do something your loved one enjoyed, such as going to the beach, listening to a style of music your loved one enjoyed, or visiting a park.
- Do something special for those who are disadvantaged. You might donate a special gift to a charity or donate money to those in need.
- Get the rest you need during these hectic times. Special events deplete your energy at the best of times, so engage in self-care.
- Do Christmas shopping well in advance to minimise stress. You don't want to be anxious and rush around with a lot of gifts to purchase.

When the grief is still raw, you are still processing the loss. Once you feel you're able to focus on things other than the loss and are slowly adapting to the absence of your loved one, you can use these strategies to help you move forward and honour the loss. Apply these strategies when you have time to yourself. Perhaps you could set a daily or weekly schedule to practise them.

PART TWO:

Personal Touch

My Personal Struggles With Grief

Our Beautiful Boy
Forever a Lasting Memory
Ingrained in our Hearts
Our Continuing Bond of Love

In 2000, my son died of a cardiac arrest at three days old at the Royal Melbourne Hospital. I found him in the incubator under the jaundice lights looking sickly pale, too pale for my liking. I opened the incubator and touched my baby, but he lay very still. I realised he wasn't breathing. My body went into shock with an unreal feeling when I turned to a nurse attending to another baby and said, "Something's wrong with my baby."

    I froze and felt like I was in a trance, another world. I don't remember exactly what my body did that morning, but I do remember almost blacking out. I do remember how my beautiful, perfect son should not have been placed underneath those lights. I do remember how I wished I was dead instead of my own innocent son.

    Within minutes, an entire group of doctors entered the nursery and attended to Jared. I was crying uncontrollably, trembling all over while a female obstetrician held my hand and told me what the doctors were doing to Jared. I kept shaking my head and saying, "No, no. He's got to be all right. He has to be all right."

    I should've been excited about taking Jared home that day. I should've had the chance to mother Jared. It should never have happened, and at that moment I blamed myself. I used so many 'what ifs' that I made myself sick with the unbearable emotional pain.

I kept saying, "If only I had come to the nursery earlier. If only he had stayed with me in the ward. If only he wasn't under those lights. If only I had taken better care of him. If only..." The list went on and on until I exhausted both my mind and body. Though he had been dead when I found him, the doctors got his heart beating again after fourteen long minutes. One doctor said he might have stopped breathing for about seven minutes, which was an awfully long time for a baby.

Jared was put into intensive care, and I went into a private room with the obstetrician, who tried her best to comfort me. My husband, Michael, and my mother arrived. They both cried at the devastating news. There was no way anyone could console us on that fateful day.

Every time I looked at Jared in intensive care, my heart broke into small fragments. My legs quivered at the sight of his poor limp body hooked up to the machines with leads spread out all over his chest to monitor his heart rate, respiration, blood pressure, and oxygen saturation. Again I cried uncontrollably, and with each tear, the nurses handed me the box of tissues I had continually used with each visit.

All we could do was touch Jared's still hands and body, so he would know he was not alone. We had no idea how long he would be comatose or if he'd ever come out of it. At times, Jared took gasping breaths called Cheyne-Stokes breaths which people do before they are about to die. It was heartbreaking to watch a perfectly healthy boy become unaware and unable to breathe on his own.

I watched Jared breathe on a ventilator, his crib covered with glad wrap to protect him from draughts from the entry door. A consultant told us Jared had lost a significant amount of oxygen to his brain. He said if Jared recovered, he'd be severely brain damaged. He said that Jared could DIE. That word alone seemed to drain all blood from my body, and a chill ran through me. I refused to believe Jared could die. It was frightening enough to be told about brain injury, but death? No, I refused to lose hope for my beautiful first-born son. This was all a nightmare I thought; just a bad dream I would soon wake up from.

On that first day, I was still in my nightgown while the nurse prepared to take Jared out of the crib. The nurse said I could hold Jared, and my heart lifted, for I missed the closeness and touch we had initially shared. Holding Jared in my arms was therapeutic as I caressed his lifeless hand and watched him fight for his precious life. Tears turned to heavy cries as I wondered why my poor innocent baby had to endure this trauma at only three days old.

Jared was put into an enclosed isolette and given medication for seizures. Despite his comatose condition, Michael and I continued to talk to him and touch him. We believed on a deep, spiritual level Jared could hear and feel us touching him. We hoped our deep abiding love could heal Jared and allow him to fight so he could come back to us as best he could.

On the 19th of May 2000, we had Jared baptised to help his condition through prayer and blessing from God. It was a special and sad day for me, because Jared was still unconscious. It was disheartening to see him unable to enjoy his baptism, a time of joyous spiritual celebration, an official ritual welcoming him into the arms of God.

I kept remembering Jared as a newborn—active with loud cries, strong, and able to breastfeed. All his senses had been intact, but now they had all vanished like a soaring bird flying further and further into the distance.

On Tuesday the 18th of July, I decided to get to the hospital later, so I could do housework to prepare for Jared's homecoming. As I was driving along the freeway, the consulting doctor from the hospital rang me. She didn't think Jared was doing too well and wondered if she should call Michael. I told her I'd be at the hospital soon, and that I'd decide then whether we needed to ring Michael. My mind was racing, and I begged God not to take Jared away from us.

When I got to the hospital, my heart broke in two when I saw my mum crying with Jared in her arms. She handed over Jared and I too started crying, because my beautiful boy looked pale, struggling with his secretions. The gasping sounds sounded worse than before, and the monitor continually beeped from his slow heart rate. I hurt not only from seeing Jared struggle, but also from seeing the profound pain in my mother's eyes.

I held Jared tightly in my arms and kissed him, telling him not to give up because he was a strong little boy who had so much to live for. He had his loving parents who would do anything for him; he had many people who loved him and wanted to see him. He had his beautiful house and nursery. He had his pram to go for rides in. He had a primary school in front of his house. He had the potential to be anything he wanted to be.

When the nurse suctioned his mouth, fresh and old blood showed up in the suction tube from the many suctions he'd already had. I knew it wasn't a good sign. Again, I berated myself for not being there at my usual time. I wanted the house to be clean when Jared came home and felt excited about the prospect.

The nurse rang Michael, and later the doctor switched off the monitor. I was glad to be rid of that annoying ring in my ears.

The social worker arrived for support while I was begging Jared not to leave us. She sat there communicating to me, but nothing anybody said could rid me of this intense, burning pain right through my heart.

My sister soon arrived and eventually held Jared. She too cried, but I had no words to give her or anyone else. I was in a deep trance, hoping this was all a nightmare I'd soon wake up from, but it wasn't.

Michael arrived about half an hour later, and we decided to take Jared home with us. If Jared was meant to die today, then we wanted him to be home. We wanted him to see his home and feel the love there. He had to see his nursery.

The Sister arrived for support. She anointed Jared and us with perfumed oil while saying a special prayer.

Waiting for the nurse to drive us home was gruelling, because she was taking an awfully long time. I was worried that Jared would die right there in the hospital, and I kept telling him to hold on because he'd soon be home.

During the trip, I continued to watch and touch Jared. My own breath stopped whenever Jared's breathing slowed down. Those sounds he made scared me, so in my mind I told God that if Jared was to die to let him die peacefully at home. We deserved that at least.

It was 2.00pm when we arrived home. I walked upstairs and showed Jared the nursery, our bedroom, and all the other rooms. At that moment, Jared wasn't making those gurgling sounds, and he didn't look so pale. He actually looked tranquil. I rocked him in the rocking chair in the nursery.

I went downstairs and held him on the couch with Michael beside me. Michael put John Lennon's music on, and Jared's song, 'Beautiful Boy' came on. We were hoping for a miracle of recovery during that song, but Jared remained peaceful and quiet.

The nurse checked his heartbeat and said it was very slow. His breathing was also slowing down. She said he was dying. I felt chills all over my body, but I still clung to hope for a miracle. Miracles happened all the time.

When the nurse checked him a second time, she said there was no heartbeat. Jared was dead and had died peacefully in Michael's arms. He died when 'Beautiful Boy' played for the second time.

I can't exactly describe the pain I felt back then. All I can tell you is it was so profound, so real. It was as if someone had stuck a knife in me and twisted the blade many times within my flesh. It was such an empty, cold, cruel feeling, as if the whole world had ended for me. There was no mercy that day, only evil and harshness, for how could a perfectly healthy little boy vanish just like that? We had waited for Jared for so long, and now he was gone.

As traumatising as the pain was, at least Jared got to see his house, away from all those machines and hospital staff. At least he died peacefully without having to suffer or struggle any longer. He had suffered long enough, and now he was resting in peace. He looked so angelic, so radiant, as if he was sleeping beautifully, imagining scenic dreams and moving beyond the physical plane that could be so cruel at times.

Jared stayed with us overnight. I put him in his cot and Michael took a few photos of him lying peacefully, as if in a state of 'Nirvana' or pure bliss. He looked so beautiful, so perfect, as if his suffering had ended.

When we were ready for bed, I took Jared out of his cot and placed him between us in bed. We said a special prayer for him and cried. We touched his body that had since become cold and a little hard. Then I put Jared back in his cot, and we both tried to get some sleep. I felt drained and fatigued, and I knew I'd probably sleep a little.

That night, I woke up at 2.00am. I felt Jared's energy and saw him in bed beside me, as if his spirit had left his body from the cot and came to comfort me. I was so sure I had seen him as if he was real. I got up, went to the nursery and checked on Jared. A part of me hoped he had miraculously woken up, but he was as he was, so I went back to bed. It was difficult going back to sleep.

When the funeral directors came to take Jared away, my parents, Michael, and I said one last goodbye. I cried again as I watched the director place him into a small bassinet and cover him. He was gone forever, but never from our hearts.

How I Moved Beyond Grief

Sometimes struggles are exactly what we need in our life. If we go through our life without any obstacles, it would cripple us. We would not be as strong as what we could have been. We could never fly (Friedrich Nietzsche).

It's been 18 years since my beautiful boy, Jared, died. I now have two daughters aged 13 and 17 and am blessed to have had all three of my children. It's difficult to really understand why Jared died, but I have a few theories. These theories have stemmed from introspection, prayer, meditation, emotional support from friends and family, and reading similar stories.

I've read stories about the spirit world and near-death experiences, so I could understand more about what happens to the soul after death. I've read stories about reincarnation and psychic powers to gain more meaning from life and be a little more reassured that death is not really the end but a mere transformation.

I've gained interest in the after-life to understand why this tragedy occurred and to know that Jared's okay in the spirit world. I believe that in his own time, Jared will come back to Earth inhabiting a different body.

Michael, my family, and I were greatly blessed to have had Jared with us for ten weeks. We could've had him for only three days, but the doctors revived him. His spirit decided to inhabit his body a little while longer.

Some mothers have miscarriages and others have a stillbirth. They never get the opportunity to be with their child, to hold them or see the colour of their eyes. We got that privilege, and for that I am eternally grateful to Jared. He kept on going because of our strong love and commitment to him, but still his mission was only temporary.

Jared's purpose or mission in life was short-lived, but he probably came down to Earth to teach us a few things. What I can tell you now is he taught us strength, to be more faithful to God and a higher being, to enjoy each day as if it was our last, to love and not judge people, to be true to ourselves and to others, and to find our spiritual purpose.

My life has changed because Jared enriched my life in many ways. He made life a blessing rather than a chore, and he's empowered me in varied aspects of my life. I've learned to live life in the present moment and to reflect upon and enjoy each day, as we never know when those we love will be taken from us. We need to spend time with friends and family, but we also need to spend time with ourselves to fill the emptiness we sometimes feel. This emptiness comes from our detachment from our very own soul.

We become so busy in our stressful, day-to-day lives that we forget who we really are and what we could be doing. This may involve spending more time with our loved ones, spending more time getting to know ourselves, or spending more time serving our community.

Jared coming into my life made me closer with my family and friends. It allowed me to delve deeper into my own soul and gain meaning from my life. Jared taught me the deepest love a mother has for her child and how one's true purpose in life is to love and fulfil our spiritual purpose.

After Jared's death, I fulfilled my spiritual purpose by meditating, spending more time with family and friends, reading tarot/oracle cards for guidance, praying, reciting affirmations, writing creatively, teaching in my job as best I could, loving everyone as best I could, and having a positive outlook on life.

Sometimes it's difficult to see other babies or children, because I imagine Jared and wonder what he would've been like had he lived. Would he have been feisty or placid? Would he have taken to strangers or not? Would he have been an openly happy child or a reserved child? I've accepted his fate, but sometimes I miss him like crazy. Yet, I know he's fine wherever he is and that God is taking amazing care of him.

Jared's death inspired me to study specialised grief counselling, and I volunteered as a grief counsellor at the Australian Centre for Grief and Bereavement for one year. I worked with grief in private practice too. I wanted to help others with what I'd been through.

Jared taught us so many things, and he'll always live on in our hearts and minds. He is not with us now, but his soul is eternal, and he'll live on this Earthly plane again. I am forever grateful to my beautiful boy, and I hope to inspire others on their life journey.

Case Studies - Grief Counselling

Following are two case studies from my work as a counsellor. For the purpose of confidentiality, I have changed my clients' names.

Serena - The Loss of Her Mother

Serena is a 28-year-old married woman with three young children, ages two, four, and seven. She came to see me because she was experiencing prolonged grief and anxiety. We had eight counselling sessions together.

While Serena was five months pregnant with her first child, her mother was diagnosed with lung cancer. She was in remission from the lung cancer when one year later, she was diagnosed with a brain tumour. Serena's mother died in 2008 after eight days in palliative care. Serena also had a family history of cancer and had lost other family members over the years.

Presenting Issues

When she came to see me, Serena was experiencing prolonged grief, panic attacks, and anxiety for about seven years. She took antidepressant medication as well as Valium as needed. Serena expressed feelings of anger due to her grief. She also reported having separation anxiety as a child.

Associated Losses or Impacts

Serena told me she had lost her heart when she lost her mother. She said, "My heart got ripped out when she died." She also lost her best friend, the closeness and communication she once had with her mother, her 'go-to' person, and her sense of security. She started having panic attacks and anxiety as a result of her mother's death.

Grieving Style

Serena had an intuitive grieving style, as she was able to talk somewhat with others about her loss and experienced emotions of sadness, yearning, and anger. She needed to develop self-confidence to be able to cope independently without her mother.

Strengths and Support System (Protective Factors)

Serena was close to her father, brother, and grandmother. She also had the support of her husband and friends. She enjoyed dance-type music, exercise, and long drives or trips with her family that helped with her emotions. She had interests in craftwork, writing, going out locally for dinner, visiting friends and family, walking, movies, and breathing or relaxation exercises. These hobbies sustained Serena, gave her a break from negative ruminations and offered a pleasurable distraction.

Counselling and Coaching Process

After learning as much as I could about Serena, I discussed her expectations and treatment plan or goals. Our objective was to better manage anxiety and panic by acknowledging and working through her grief issues using a range of strategies. Serena wanted to feel freer to leave the house and not worry about having a panic attack.

We discussed what had worked for her thus far, and she mentioned that movement or exercise helped, as well as distraction and changing her self-talk. She'd seen a counsellor before, so had some insight into tools that were effective.

We spoke about general self-care that included increasing hydration, grazing on healthy foods, and learning more about the psychology of anxiety and grief. Serena read about grief models and completed a thought and emotion record, another tool she could use to challenge thoughts that usually resulted in panic and anxiety.

We explored Serena's secondary losses, and I offered her the opportunity to engage in her emotions and thoughts of grief using her body and mindfulness practices.

Serena engaged in things that her mother liked. For example, she made rice pudding, which was one of her mother's favourite foods.

As her mother's birthday came up, Serena and I brainstormed ways to manage this day. Serena found a grief poem on the Internet that gave her comfort. She created a shrine in her home that consisted of a battery-operated candle and a photo of her mother. On her mother's birthday, Serena spent time at the shrine and ate a cupcake in honour of her mother.

We worked with several Shadow Cards (see the resources section for more detail) to get further in touch with Serena's emotions related to grieving. Serena used Strengths Cards (also described in more detail in the resource section) to manage her grief and anxiety as well.

I also showed Serena how to use a fear hierarchy. I had her list things she feared from lowest level of fear to highest level of fear and practice the easiest activities first. It was crucial to explore these fears so she could combat her anxiety and begin facing things. For instance, she was able to face a crowd at a busy time in the grocery store and felt a little anxiety but was not overwhelmed by it.

I guided Serena in visualisation exercises to relax her mind and body. We also brainstormed ways to distract her thoughts such as undertaking practical, hands-on tasks or leisure activities, and practising breathing exercises. Serena brought in a photo of her mother and shared memories with me. Serena also decided she would watch the movies, Ghost and Beaches to understand grief.

Serena created a memory box and filled it with mementoes and items that reminded her of her mother, including photos, funeral cards, candles, and other sentimental items. Creating this box allowed Serena to maintain a connection or bond with her mother and keep memories of her mother alive.

Outcomes

Serena was able to explore her fears and stop avoiding places that had made her anxious or reminded her of her mother. She was able to better manage her grief and not be overwhelmed when thinking about her mother. She was no longer trapped in her grief, thus no longer letting it prevent her from living her life.

Serena was better able to manage her anxiety and face crowds in the grocery store and at family events. She was able to take longer drives beyond her local area. She reported feeling stronger within herself and wanted to continue being strong. She no longer had panic attacks, despite still feeling a little anxiety.

Anna - The Loss of Her Husband

I worked with Anna at the Australian Centre for Grief and Bereavement several years ago. She came to six weekly counselling sessions and later participated in family interventions at a hospital.

Anna was a 39-year-old female whose husband Ned had died from melanoma in 2013 at age 42. At the time, Anna, her three children, ages eight, six and two years, and her husband Ned had lived for three years in San Francisco, where Ned was vice president of a large company.

Ned was previously a lawyer. They met at university when Anna was in her first year of law and Ned was in his third year. Anna was twenty-one years old when she met Ned. They had been married for eleven years and had known each other for seventeen years when Ned died.

Anna's father had died of pancreatic cancer, and he was in agony for almost two years. Ned helped Anna grieve for her father. It was a devastating loss, as she was very close to her father. Anna's paternal grandfather had died of lung cancer.

Anna had given up her job when her son was two years old, six years before she started counselling.

Family History

In the United States there was a new drug for melanoma, but Ned didn't qualify for the drug trial, which would have given him a 52 percent chance of survival. Anna had campaigned to get the melanoma drug and got 500,000 signatures on a petition. She was still unable to access the drug.

Ned was sick for two years, but he still enjoyed playing football and was active. In the end, he had a stroke.

In Singapore, where they had lived for three years prior to living in the USA, Ned saw a doctor for the moles on his back. He was diagnosed with melanoma in 2009 in Singapore. Some moles were cut out. Then in the United States, Anna told Ned to see the company doctor about other moles. The doctor said the moles were fine. Then he saw a skin specialist who had moles removed and said there was a 95 percent chance he was fine. Anna suspected two moles that remained on his back had killed him. He grew up on a farm and was constantly in the sun without sunscreen. Anna was very angry about this, particularly knowing that his mother was a nurse and should have known better.

Anna's mother was German with a strong disciplinary style, but her father had a softer personality. She connected more closely to her father than her mother.

Presenting Issues

Anna struggled to accept her husband's death and wanted to better manage her emotions. She had lived overseas for a while, so needed to adjust to Melbourne again. Anna also had anger management issues. She was angry towards her family and her husband (for leaving her, which is quite normal in cases of grief).

Anna also worried somewhat about the genetic component of cancer and wanted her children to get tested by a specialist.

Associated Losses or Impacts

Anna reported losing her financial security and her love of San Francisco, which she described as a place with friendly people. She also missed her friendships and abundant support in San Francisco as she had left a lot of friends there. Furthermore, she had lost her sense of meaning and purpose as she considered Ned her meaning and purpose. She had lost her soul mate.

Grieving Style

Anna was more instrumental in her grieving style as she tended to cry alone and found that others didn't understand her great loss. She was unable to talk to others about Ned.

Strengths and Support System

Anna's sister and mother helped her out with her children, but she was not very close to them. Her mother babysat her children as needed. Anna had a couple of friends in Melbourne and the support of her late husband's friends. She also enjoyed exercise, yoga, reading, and writing.

Counselling and Coaching Process

Anna's objectives in counselling were to accept her husband's death and better manage her emotions and level of resilience. She also needed to readjust to the Melbourne lifestyle. Anna wanted to find meaning and purpose in her life as well. She wanted to access new support or improve her current support systems.

In the first session, I validated and assured her that her anger towards the death and family members was normal. I suggested ways she could communicate with her mother about her mother's disciplinary style with Anna's children and assertively ask for what she needed to be supported. For example, she needed her mother to encourage her to attend counselling, and she needed to communicate her needs to her family and friends who brought food she didn't need.

I helped Anna understand the Dual Process Model of grief which explained how to grieve, feel, and cry some of the time and get on with things at other times. In other words, she could focus on her emotions versus do day-to-day practical tasks.

We explored secondary losses or impacts of the death, allowing her to give expression to unnamed emotions, particularly by writing down some of her emotions as a way of containing them.

We explored her relationship with Ned and what he appreciated about her, which was her sweetness and their good intellectual conversations.

We explored her early relationship with her parents and sister. She spoke to her sister about talking to her mother about Anna's need for her mother to be more supportive with Anna's children rather than yelling at them. Anna thought her mother was too disciplinary in style.

We spoke about planning Father's Day. We discussed rituals in general and ideas for specific activities. We brainstormed activities Anna felt she could do on Father's Day. For example, she could light a candle and go to the football, which was what Ned had enjoyed. Anna ended up buying a plant in honour of Ned on Father's Day, and this maintained her connection and bond with her late husband.

Anna and I also discussed goals and self-care, including quiet time for writing or reading and respite from her children so she could re-establish her identity without Ned.

By moving beyond grief to find meaning, we explored Anna's previous purpose and enjoyment in life whilst growing up, apart from her duties as a wife and mother. She stated she had enjoyed school and schoolwork, got high marks and was independent. Anna reported having friends and being social. She was academic and became a corporate lawyer. She discovered writing gave her meaning and purpose, and she previously wrote fiction. Her children gave her purpose, but she was lonely and had to do everything herself without her husband.

We further explored Anna's purpose using Strength Cards, and she chose 'I can choose to be resilient' and 'I can choose to be calm.' She considered getting involved with the Olivia Newton John Cancer Centre due to her previous campaign for the melanoma drug. Anna knew how to help others with treatment, particularly less aggressive immunotherapy, which turns on the immune system and is less aggressive than chemotherapy or radiotherapy. A friend of Anna's husband had called her and suggested she get involved in the cancer centre. This involvement in raising awareness of melanoma would allow her to make sense of her loss and be resilient in her grief.

Anna also decided to be in a calm place when her children went to bed. She could have a cup of tea and enjoy her quiet time while reflecting on her life purpose and future.

Outcomes

Anna was able to cry openly in the session, becoming more of an intuitive griever and sharing her grief. She was proactive in talking to her mother and sister about needing help with her children. She enlisted the help of her mother with financial matters relating to Ned's accounts and superannuation.

Anna used her strengths and coping strategies, including reading, yoga, exercise, and writing fiction again, to gain pleasure and mastery from life. She became more optimistic, possibly due to securing much better support from her mother after her sister had spoken to her mother, and by speaking to the doctor about specialist referrals for cancer tests.

PART THREE:

Solutions for Moving Beyond Grief

How to Use and Build Your Inner Strengths

Self-compassion is kindness to yourself when you feel you're going crazy after a loss. Assuring yourself that a range of feelings around loss are normal can help you build strength and patience with your grieving process.

Self-compassion, as discussed by Kristin Neff, is being kind and gentle with yourself when you make mistakes or notice personal flaws. Rather than criticising and judging yourself for weaknesses, you are understanding and treat yourself the way you'd treat a good friend.

Practising self-compassion takes time and persistence and can improve the way you feel about yourself. Here are a couple of exercises from self-compassion.org that I have practised myself and with clients, particularly when I'm beating myself up.

Exercise – Journal of Self-Compassion

Part One – Write about an issue that makes you feel inadequate. It could involve work, self-image, or relationships. Think about the feelings you have when you consider this part of your life. Allow your emotions to come up as they are and write about them.

Part Two – Now write a letter to yourself from the perspective of a loving friend who accepts you unconditionally. This friend sees all your strengths and weaknesses, including the part of your life you just wrote about. Think about what this friend feels towards you and how your friend loves and accepts you for who you are with all your imperfections. Your friend knows your past and understands how you are in this moment. Your weakness is related to a range of things outside your control, including genetics, family history, and life experiences.

What would this friend say about your weakness? How would this friend explain the strong compassion he or she feels for you and for the pain you feel when you criticise yourself? Your friend would say you are only human and that all of us have strengths and weaknesses. What changes would your friend suggest in terms of compassion and unconditional love?

As you write this letter, get a sense of a strong acceptance, kindness, gentleness and your need for general well-being.

Part Three – After writing the letter, set it aside for a while. Then read it again and allow your body to absorb the words. Allow yourself to feel the compassion that comforts you. You deserve to feel loved, connected, and accepted.

Exercise – How Would You Treat A Friend?

Cast your mind back to when a friend felt bad about him or herself and was going through a hard time. Write down what you'd normally say and do and the tone you use with friends.

Now think about moments you felt bad about yourself or were having a hard time. How do you normally respond in these moments? Write down what you usually say and do. Identify the tone you use to talk to yourself. Was there a difference? If yes, why? What causes you to treat yourself differently from others?

Self-compassion is essential for happiness and general well-being. You can feel things but be gentle with yourself. Treat yourself as though you're speaking to your inner child.

Here are more exercises to enrich your level of self-compassion, and hence, happiness. You can use them to reflect on your life and react to your human frailties with more compassion and comfort.

Self-Compassion Journal

Keep a daily journal for one week, longer, or for life. Journalling helps you articulate your feelings and tends to improve your mental and physical well-being. At the end of the day, you can review what happened during that day, then write about this in your journal. Write about things that didn't go well, any self-judgements, or any distress you experienced. For example, you might have got angry with a friend because she said something hurtful. Later, you felt guilty and ashamed for lashing out at your friend and may find a way to apologise. For each experience, use mindfulness and kindness to reflect on the experience in a more self-compassionate manner. Be accepting without judgement about your experiences.

Validate that your experiences were part of the larger world, telling yourself humans are not perfect and it's natural to have experiences that hurt. Think about what caused the experience and the circumstances. Perhaps an event triggered painful memories. Again, be kind to yourself.

Self-Compassion Break

Ponder a situation in your life that is challenging and creating stress. Experience the situation by feeling the stress and physical sensations in your body. You might feel tight in the chest or have pain in your stomach as you think about the situation. Now tell yourself:

This situation brings me suffering.
Suffering is the way life is.
Then place your hands over your heart, feeling the warm sensation and comforting touch of your hands on your chest.
Tell yourself 'May I be safe. May I be peaceful. May I be kind to myself. May I accept myself the way I am.'

Changing Your Critical Self-Talk

Changing your critical self-talk is about working with your inner critic. You may do this in your journal over a few weeks to help you relate to yourself in a self-compassionate way. Firstly, you need to identify when you are criticising yourself. Focus on a negative experience and notice what you've told yourself about the experience. Is there a pattern or a theme to your critical voice? Is it the voice of a parent or someone else from your past? Your voice might be saying, 'Why did you eat a whole bag of chips? You're hopeless!'

Identify when you criticise yourself and soften the inner critic with compassion. Tell your critical voice you appreciate the concern, but the voice is hurting you rather than helping you. Then let your compassionate self-speak.

With self-compassion, you can look at the situation differently by saying something like 'I know you ate the bag of chips, but you were feeling stressed, and food gives you comfort. Maybe next time, you could write in your journal, go for a walk, or find other simple, non-fattening pleasures that give you comfort. What would a compassionate friend tell you about this situation? As you reframe the situation, comfort yourself physically by stroking your heart or arm. Bring up those emotions of gentleness, kindness, and support.

Another great exercise you can do to discover your strengths is ask friends and family what they see as your positive qualities.

For a FREE test on discovering your top five strengths, you can peruse this website about positive psychology: www.authentichappiness.sas.upenn.edu. To get to your free test, click on **Questionnaires**, then click on '**Brief Strengths Test**.' You will need to sign in to create a free account.

External Resources for Grief and Loss

Here is a list of resources you can use to help you in your grief journey:
- Grief support groups and grief associations (there is a list at the end of this book).
- Books about emotions or practical matters related to grief, suited to both intuitive and instrumental grievers.
- Online resources about personal stories or grief in general.
- Creative arts, including painting, drawing, listening to music, photography, journalling, scrapbooking, or writing poetry.
- Counsellors, coaches, or psychologists who can help you look deeper into your issues or help you envision your ideal self and move forward towards goals.

Creating a Vision of Wellness or Fulfillment

A vision statement describes a change you desire for the future or how you see your ideal self. The vision statement tends to increase holistic health and hope and gives you strong motivation to move forward. You can see beyond your present life to create what doesn't yet exist.

The vision statement discusses what you want (outcomes), why you want it (values), what could get in the way (obstacles), and what you're able to do to overcome these obstacles (strategies).

A vision draws on wellness, which is the existence of well-being or living life well in all areas of your life. The National Wellness Institute states, *"Wellness is the process of becoming aware of and making choices towards a more successful existence."*

In other words, you can achieve wellness by utilising a range of steps that give you control over your behaviour so you can reach the desired state. Your vision gives you strong, positive feelings, motivation, excitement, health, fulfillment, and vitality.

Motivation is a compelling reason to create change. Knowing why you wish to change will help you stay on track. For example, you might want to lose ten kilograms because you'd like to be active with your children.

If you'd like to change because of external motivators rather than internal motivators (your mother is forcing you to lose weight), your vision will not create sustainable change. You need to be motivated for you own compelling reasons rather than what you feel you 'should' do. This motivation ties in with your values. The vision is your driver to change when it aligns with values that give you a sense of meaning and purpose in life.

Here is an example of a vision statement: "I would like to have more energy and optimism in my life (what) so I can perform more daily tasks, be a good role model for my children, and be more patient with people (why). My greatest obstacle is my difficulty with sleep (obstacle). I can read and learn about sleep tips and reduce my caffeine intake to improve my sleep routine (strategy). I am quite determined and resilient and have an optimistic view of life (strength)."

When creating a vision statement, ask yourself the following questions:
1. What would you like to achieve in one area of your life (for example, weight loss, increase in energy, more exercise, better nutrition, lower stress, other health issues or behaviours)?
2. Why is this change important to you?
3. What else might change as a result of this vision?
4. What is your greatest obstacle?
5. What are some strategies to overcome your obstacle?

Goal-Setting -SMART

It's crucial to turn your VISION into action and reality by setting clear goals that entail the following:
Specific: Make the goal as specific as possible so you have clarity about what to do.
Measurable: Set a goal you can measure so you know when you have achieved it.
Action-Based: Break down your vision into a set of behaviours you will do consistently for three months. You can set weekly goals as stepping stones to the goals you wish to achieve in three months.
Realistic: Set goals that are achievable so you're likely to complete the goal. Successfully reaching one goal leads to success with other goals. It also builds your confidence.
Time-Bound: Establish a timeframe for reaching your goals, whether it's three months or a week.

As an example of the above, you might wish to set three-month goals that include:
1. *I will be riding my bike to work three times a week in three months' time. My weekly goal to help me reach that outcome is I will ride my bike around the block on Monday evening, then gradually increase the time over the weeks.*
2. *I will have lost at least ten kilograms in three months' time. My weekly goal to help me reach that outcome is I will research healthy eating and exercise routines this week.*

In order to attain your weekly and three-monthly goals, you can enlist the support of friends and family or have an accountability partner to keep you on track. You can ask your support system for what you need. For instance, if your goal is to lose weight, you might ask that your mother not buy any sweets for the family.

You can also get support from coaching programs, counsellors, or groups. You might need a personal trainer or a wellness coach. You might need a counsellor. You might even join the gym or attend a support group.

Your level of confidence in reaching your goals is important. If your level of confidence is a seven out of ten, you are more likely to succeed with that goal. If it's lower than seven, you might need to review your goals and change the goal completely. Each productive step leads you to more and more success.

Commitment is also important to reaching your goals. You can write down your goals and remind yourself of your vision and why it's so important for you to reach your goal. Stay aligned with your true values and commit to your action steps.

You will encounter obstacles along the way, so problem-solving is crucial for success as well. Prior to acting on your goal, you need to have strategies that will help you overcome obstacles and challenges. By combating things that get in the way, you'll build your confidence for any future challenges. Remind yourself of how you handled a similar situation or goal in the past.

Reviews are gold to authors and allow Lucy to keep writing. If you enjoyed this book, please consider rating and reviewing it on Amazon: http://mybook.to/MovingBeyondGrief

Conclusion

As a qualified counsellor and writer, I have researched, worked, and trained in the areas of grief and holistic health. I have had clients who were bereaved by suicide, parental loss, child loss, spousal loss, and the loss of a missing person. I have also counselled clients who had lost something of value, such as a job role, a relationship, their identity, or their functional health, and who all grieved in their own special way. It has been rewarding to assist those experiencing such personal loss.

I hope you have drawn inspiration from these ideas and case studies and that you are able to move forward to a life of joy and purpose.

I no longer have a private counselling practice but do manage to solve problems in my romantic suspense novels. My fiction novels focus on strong women who have endured grief, loss, and trauma. My female protagonists show resilience when overcoming personal challenges, and I base my characters on aspects of my own personality and on others that I know.

I wish you the best of luck!

Books/Resources

J. William Worden (2009)
Grief Counselling and Grief Therapy - A Handbook for the Mental Health Practitioner -Fourth Edition

Kenneth J. Doka & Terry L. Martin (2010)
Grieving Beyond Gender

Kristin Neff (self-compassion)
https://self-compassion.org/

Leah Giarratano, (2004)
Managing Psychological Trauma

Mal McKissock and Dianne McKissock (2012)
Coping with Grief - The Trusted Classic Guide for the Bereaved and Their Loved Ones

Edited by Robert A. Neimeyer *(2012)*
Techniques of Grief Therapy - Counselling Practices for Counselling the Bereaved

Russ Harris (2011)
The Reality Slap - How To Find Fulfilment When Life Hurts

Resources for the Community

Australian Centre for Grief and Bereavement - Offers bereavement counselling, support groups, and information for wide-ranging groups, as well as education, and workshops for professionals.
https://www.grief.org.au/

Grief Link - Offers information about grief to professionals and the community.
http://www.grieflink.asn.au/

Australian Child & Adolescent Trauma, Loss and Grief Network - a network that increases awareness of trauma, loss and grief for this group.
https://emergingminds.com.au/about/who-we-are/

Support After Suicide - Provides resources, support groups, and counselling to those impacted by suicide and education and training for professionals.
http://www.supportaftersuicide.org.au/

Overcoming Grief - A Self-Help Guide Using Cognitive Behavioural Techniques
by Sue Morris, 2008

Shadow Cards - to purchase
https://innovativeresources.org/resources/card-sets/shadows-and-deeper-shadows/

Strength Cards - to purchase
https://innovativeresources.org/resources/card-sets/choosing-strengths/

ABOUT THE AUTHOR

Lucy Appadoo is a prolific reader and author of the Friends In Crisis Series. After a childhood spent reading and imagining escapist worlds, Lucy has put her imagination into stories. Her work as a rehabilitation counsellor, and former work as a counsellor in private practice, have led to an interest in writing inspirational stories about authentic, driven women who manage adversity with strength and heart. She writes in the genres of romantic suspense/thrillers with significant life themes and contemporary romance.

Lucy's interests include researching crime stories and news to inspire her work, watching crime thrillers and suspenseful movies, travel, exercising, reading for entertainment or knowledge, meditation, and spending time with friends and family. She also appreciates her Italian background and culture, which has inspired her to write imaginative stories about her parents' childhoods, leading to The Italian Family Series novels.

Check out Lucy's website and sign up for a FREE romantic suspense novel here: www.lucyappadooauthor.com.au

ALSO BY LUCY APPADOO

NON-FICTION

Stress Management & Anxiety
Holistic Spiritual and Mental Health - Building Resilience and Creativity by Conquering Anxiety and Managing Stress - http://mybook.to/Holistichealth

Career Guidance
Your Holistic Career Path - Create Career Change, Satisfaction, and Work/Life Balance - http://mybook.to/YourHolisticCareerPath

Journal and Record Of Books You've Read (with Quotes)
Readers' Journal - http://mybook.to/ReadersJournal

FICTION

The Friends In Crisis Series - Romantic Suspense/Thriller
Haunted By The Past (Book 1) -
http://mybook.to/HauntedbythePast
Twisted Obsession (Book 2) -
http://mybook.to/TwistedObsession
Web Of Lies (Book 3) - http://mybook.to/EbookWebOfLies

The Hearts Series - Romantic Suspense
Rising Hearts (Book 1) - http://mybook.to/RisingHearts
Forbidden Hearts (Book 2) -
http://mybook.to/ForbiddenHearts
Kindred Hearts - (Book 3) - http://mybook.to/kindredhearts
Broken Hearts (prequel to Forbidden Hearts) -
http://mybook.to/Bhearts

Short Story Thrillers
Evening Interrupted - http://mybook.to/Eveninginterrupted
The Dreamcatcher - http://viewbook.at/Thedreamcatcher
Red Flags - http://mybook.to/Redflags
Collection of Short Story Thrillers -
http://mybook.to/collectionofthrillers

The Italian Family Series - Coming of Age Family Drama/Romance
A New Life - http://mybook.to/ANewLife
The Beauty of Tears - http://mybook.to/TheBeautyofTears
Dancing in the Rain - http://mybook.to/dancingintheRain
A Life By Design - http://mybook.to/Alifebydesign

www.ingramcontent.com/pod-product-compliance
Lightning Source LLC
Chambersburg PA
CBHW072114290426
44110CB00014B/1911